D1361627

Design: Todd Bates
Editorial: Brian Arundel
Production Coordination: Shirley Woo
Project Management: Sheila Kamuda

Cover Photographs: (top) David Vaughn, (bottom) © Envision/Corbis

Library of Congress Cataloging-in-Publication Data
Skinner, Angela.
Race day grub: recipes from the NASCAR family / by Angela Skinner.
p. cm.
Includes index.
ISBN-13: 978-0-470-09858-5 (cloth)
1. Cookery, American. 2. Stock car drivers--United States. 3. NASCAR (Association) I. Title.
TX715.S6356 2006
641.5'973--dc22
200602055

10 9 8 7 6 5 4 3 2 1

Manufactured in China

Officially Licensed by

RACE DAY GRUB

RECIPES FROM THE NASCAR FAMILY

BY ANGELA SKINNER

BICENTENNIAL
1807
WILEY
2007
BICENTENNIAL

CHAPTER FOUR: SLICK SIDES AND SALADS

CHAPTER FIVE: SWEET VICTORIES—DESSERTS

CHAPTER SIX: RACING KIDS

CHAPTER SEVEN: SPIRITS AND WHISTLE-WETTERS

FOREWORD

by Mike Skinner

In my thirty years of racing, I've had the opportunity to see a lot of tailgating, and I've done my fair share of eating. When you are on the road as much as I am, it's easy to go out to a restaurant, but it's much more enjoyable eating a home-cooked meal at the race track, enjoying the atmosphere of your campsite—after all, that's part of the experience of a NASCAR weekend.

When Angie and I first started dating, I couldn't quite figure out why she always wanted to go out to eat. I had a beautiful motor coach that was equipped with a modern kitchen, yet we constantly made reservations at restaurants. Because I was trying to romance her at the time, I didn't want to rock the boat, so I kept agreeing. It didn't take long, though, for me to figure it out—after she exploded a few hot dogs in the microwave and burned a few fillets, I realized that she couldn't cook!

Once I discovered her bluff, I decided to grill our dinners myself, while she cooked the side dishes. Although I think it killed her ego to do so, Angie tackled the job. I admit that for a while we ate chicken and cheesy rice casserole, or chicken and pasta marinated in Italian dressing just about every weekend, but Angie quickly learned what cooking was all about. These days, I'm lucky if she lets me barbecue a steak—and that's only after she spent the afternoon preparing it.

It didn't take Angie long to become a fantastic cook, and because of our lifestyle, she's also become a master of making delicious meals in twenty minutes. When you read this book, not only will you get a lot of great suggestions for good, sit-down meals, but also a lot of quick and simple ideas and recipes that

you will absolutely love. You will also get to enjoy my wife's wonderful personality and wit as she presents these recipes in a comical yet admiring manner, capturing the stories behind each dish.

If you want to see how NASCAR celebrities, their spouses, and their friends prepare their favorite weekend dishes, start reading Race Day Grub. Pick out your next favorite recipe, sit down with the beverage of your choice, and start cooking!

///NASCAR

INTRODUCTION

"Isn't life on the road rough?" That's the number one question I get asked by hundreds of fans and friends while supporting my husband, Mike, on the NASCAR circuit. I often laugh to myself because actually I love all the traveling! It's pretty hard to not enjoy driving all around the country when you get to stay in the comfort of your own motor coach.

I used to stay in hotel rooms and eat every meal out when I traveled. But after I joined the madness and excitement of NASCAR racing, I immediately started to collect healthy recipes that I could make for us in our motor coach. Unfortunately, I couldn't cook a lick! In order to impress Mike, I had to learn. I actually started a handwritten cookbook—which I gathered by calling my sister, mother, and gran about ten times a week!

I think I reached the peak of my embarrassment when Mike suggested that I cook a turkey for Christmas Eve in 1999. I had cheated for Thanksgiving by calling my mother and convincing her to drive from Ohio to North Carolina just to cook the turkey and make the gravy. I figured I would cheat at Christmas by buying a ham! When Mike requested a Christmas turkey, I panicked. Early Christmas Eve morning, he caught me with a telephone in each ear: On one, my sister was explaining how to clean a turkey; on the other, my mother was teaching me how to make gravy. I bought the wrong size pan for the turkey, and I ended up having to cut the wings off of the massive bird so it would fit in the roasting pan. At this point Mike finally said, "I thought you knew how to cook?" The only thing I knew to do was just start laughing. So we both burst into laughter and I had my racing husband help me butter up the bird and throw it in a new pan. We laughed even harder when the turkey slid across the granite countertop and nearly fell on the floor. The dinner turned out fabulously and no one at the table knew the trouble I went through, but I decided on that day to learn to cook. Today, cooking is one of my favorite hobbies, and I love to hear the words "Thank you honey, that was awesome!"

I agree with the saying that variety is the spice of life—especially when it comes to food! I get tired of the same old hotdog-and-hamburger cookout every weekend. Now I find myself entertaining our race team, along with friends and competitors, all the time, whether it's with after-work drinks and some quick and tasty appetizers, or at the picnic table for a full-course meal outdoors.

You can pretty much make anything on the road, but finding easy and enjoyable recipes is a challenge. And you don't want to spend all your time in the kitchen while you're on your vacation or taking in the excitement of a NASCAR race. Also, when you're cooking in your RV, you have to think about conserving water, creating a complete meal on a tiny stove, and coming up with quick and efficient cleaning tricks.

To put this book together, I set out to "invite" myself to a few race-related dinner parties, and I came back with some great new recipes to try out on my husband and our race team. Some of the touching and hilarious stories the conributors shared were as good as the meals. If you ask me, the perfect recipe is when you can tempt the tummy of a new friend and take in a thrilling NASCAR race all in one afternoon.

When I started to collect recipes from our NASCAR family, I had limited my collecting to the drivers and crewmembers. Then I realized some of the best "grillmeisters" were the diehard NASCAR fans, camping out in the infield every weekend of the race season. Many fans come with elaborate setups for their campsites, and annual traditions that would rival the tailgating in any other sport. Our fans are extraordinarily loyal, and they always welcome new fans to join in on the fun.

Each weekend we all—the drivers, their families, the race crews and, of course, the fans—gather at a track as one big NASCAR family, and the meals and time spent together capture the ultimate experience of a NASCAR race. In *Race Day Grub*, you will find very simple and typical fare, as well as some very creative variations of your favorite foods, gathered from the South, the North, and the West Coast. I even jotted down a few tips for speeding up your meal preparation, and some little lessons I've learned to make your food taste great and cook properly.

If you want to experience some of the atmosphere of one of the most popular spectator sports in America, start turning the pages and sample these culinary creations from the folks who make the NASCAR experience possible almost every weekend of the year.

CHAPTER ONE

RACE MORNING BREAKFASTS

Starting off the day with a filling breakfast is a must for most race-car drivers. Most NASCAR races begin around noon, so the drivers, crews, and families don't get the chance to eat lunch. Because the races also last four to six hours, getting "fueled-up" in the morning is an absolute necessity. To get yourself off to a good start, try these fabulous ideas for how to wave your own green flag!

SKINNERITE BREAKFAST CASSEROLE

The fans of Mike Skinner are a pretty tight group, and they try to get together at almost every race. Every year they gather near California and even throw a toga party, where they dress up a cardboard stand-up image of Mike. It was easy, then, to request a few of their favorite meals. This one happens to be one of my favorites because it captures the creativity of our diehard fans and includes one of Mike's favorite ingredients: sausage!

INGREDIENTS:

1 pound bulk sausage
One 8-ounce can refrigerated crescent dinner rolls
2 cups shredded Cheddar or mozzarella cheese
4 large eggs, beaten

¾ cup milk
¼ teaspoon salt
⅛ teaspoon pepper

PREPARATION:

Preheat the oven to 425°F.

In a large skillet, brown the sausage over medium heat. Drain well on paper towels.

Line the bottom of a greased 13-by-9-by-2-inch baking pan with the crescent dinner rolls, pressing the perforations to seal. Sprinkle the sausage and cheese over the dinner rolls.

Combine the eggs, milk, salt, and pepper. Beat well and pour over the sausage and cheese. Bake 15 minutes. Let stand for 5 minutes and cut into squares for serving.

Makes 6 to 8 servings.

THE LAZY
MEAT AND EGG BAKE

One race day morning I decided I wanted an omelet for breakfast, but I really didn't want to stand over the stove flipping and paying close attention to a soft, fluffy-egg breakfast. So I came up with this semi-quiche—a lazy way to make an omelet pie. I guess the fancy name for this is a frittata, but I like my name better.

INGREDIENTS:

1 pound bulk sausage
1 small onion, diced
6 large eggs
Splash of milk
1 ½ cup shredded sharp Cheddar cheese
1 small can sliced mushrooms (or ½ cup fresh mushrooms, sliced)
1 teaspoon garlic powder
½ teaspoon salt
½ teaspoon pepper
Hot pepper sauce and toast, for serving

PREPARATION:

Preheat the oven to 375°F.

In a large skillet, brown the sausage over medium heat. When the sausage is halfway cooked through, stir in the diced onion.

While the sausage cooks, beat the eggs with a whisk or fork and add a splash of milk.

Remove the cooked sausage from the skillet and place on paper towels to drain. Add the sausage mixture to the egg mixture. Add the cheese, mushrooms, garlic powder, salt, and pepper. Blend all the ingredients together and pour into a greased, 9-by-2-inch round glass baking dish.

Bake for 25 to 30 minutes.

Slice and serve with a little hot sauce and toast!

Makes 4 to 6 servings.

Like most NASCAR fans, diehard Skinnerites are far from bashful about identifying their favorite driver.

HEART ATTACK ON A PLATE

Henry Benfield might be the most outrageous character in the NASCAR garage. Mr. Benfield has driven a few race cars himself, along with a few race haulers for teams. He's also served on many pit crews and has cooked for most of us in the garage at one time or another. Henry's been around for many years and can share a lot of great stories, but now it's time for me to tattle on him a little.

When I first started attending NASCAR races, Henry was one of the first to greet me, and the first to offer me a sandwich—it was his "Heart Attack on a Plate" creation, and it was delicious. I thought everything was great until a few amused friends warned me that I should be more aware of Henry's cooking.

Apparently Henry has taught a few rude garage guards a lesson or two. For example, one hot summer day in Richmond a guard was a little smart with Henry, so Henry decided to make his special lemonade—containing a few special drops of citrus magnesium. The rest of the afternoon the guard stayed locked inside the port-o-john, and practically everyone ended up in the garage! The next guard who treated Henry somewhat rudely ended up with some Ex-Lax brownies. You can imagine why some folks are a little hesitant to taste Henry's meals, but the only questionable step that I noticed was how he cleaned his skillet. I guess a little SD-20 never hurt anyone, though.

14

INGREDIENTS:

1 tablespoon butter
1 green bell pepper, sliced
1 red bell pepper, sliced
1 onion, sliced
1-2 large eggs

1 tablespoon mayonnaise
2 slices of white bread
1 slice American cheese
1 teaspoon powdered garlic

PREPARATION:

Heat the butter in a skillet and cook the peppers and onions over medium heat, stirring, until softened, about 5 minutes. Remove from the skillet and set aside. In the same skillet, fry the eggs until hard. Remove the eggs from the skillet and set aside.

Spread mayonnaise on one side of the bread slices. Add more butter to the skillet and brown the bread (use the side without mayonnaise).

While the bread is browning, place the cheese on one slice and top with the eggs. Add the peppers and onions and sprinkle with garlic powder.

Once the bread is browned and the cheese is melted, remove from skillet and make a sandwich. Serve quickly.

Makes 1 serving.

GRANDMA RED'S BISCUITS AND GRAVY

This recipe came from our nephew Paul, who still resides in Northern California, but it originated with Mike's mother. Everyone called her "Red" for her striking hair and feisty personality—sound like any race-car driver you know? She also claimed bragging rights for this usually southern-style meal, declaring, "It's best in the West." She may have given the southern boys a running! Grandma Red used to make this breakfast all the time for her grandson Paul, as well as for her little boy, Mike Skinner.

INGREDIENTS:

Bisquick mix
One 16-ounce package Jimmy Dean spicy sausage, ground
2-3 cups milk
4 tablespoons flour
Salt
Pepper

PREPARATION:

Make 4 to 6 biscuits by following the directions on the back of the Bisquick box.

Cook the sausage in a skillet over medium heat until brown, breaking into small crumbs.

Mix together 2 cups of milk and the flour; set aside.

When the sausage is done, keep the skillet hot and pour the milk-flour mixture over the cooked sausage. Stir well. After 2 to 3 minutes, reduce the heat while continuously stirring, and add about 1 cup milk until the gravy reaches the desired thickness. (The gravy will be pretty thick—if you want thinner gravy, just keep adding more milk.)

Add salt and pepper to taste, and pour the gravy over the biscuits.

Makes 4 to 6 servings.

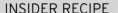

CHAPTER TWO

SPEEDY STARTERS AND SNACKS

Appealing appetizers and snacks to munch on throughout the day are probably my favorite foods to prepare. Sometimes I just make an assortment of dips and appetizers for our race team to eat after a long day in the NASCAR garage. If you are entertaining your friends at home or at your campsite, you should always have a fun "starter" to offer. And you'll love these ideas because most of them can be prepared in less than twenty minutes—because you need to take in the race too, not be stuck in the kitchen!

SMOKE'S SHRIMP

When I started collecting recipes from my peers in the NASCAR garage, I noticed that two-time NASCAR NEXTEL Cup Champion Tony Stewart had a new barbeque sauce out on the market. The sauce was named after Tony's nickname out on the race track—"Smoke"—and it's almost as good as Tony's driving!

Tony asked me to create a recipe using his new sauce for this book, and this is my creation. I tested it on a few Craftsman Truck Series drivers and a number of NASCAR reporters during a media function. It was the most popular dish at the event, and I even created a lot of smoke on my own while cooking it on the grill! My suggestion is to grill these wonderful treats on LOW—or you may end up smoking out all your guests, like I did.

INGREDIENTS:

1 pound fresh large shrimp, peeled and deveined (tails on)
Pepper
Garlic powder
Dried onion flakes
12-ounce package bacon

Toothpicks
One 18-ounce jar barbeque sauce
   (try Smoke's Bar-B-Que sauce,
    found at www.smoke20.com)

PREPARATION:

Clean the shrimp and rinse under cold water in a colander. Pat dry. Season the shrimp with pepper, garlic powder and onion flakes to taste.

Cut the bacon slices in half and wrap half a bacon strip around each shrimp, securing with toothpick. Place the shrimp in a shallow glass pan and pour the barbeque sauce evenly over all of the shrimp. Cover with aluminum foil or plastic wrap and marinate in the refrigerator for 1 hour.

Prepare a grill. Grill the shrimp over low heat until the bacon begins to crisp. Be careful to not overcook!

Makes 4 to 6 servings.

I know this is lazy, but I really dislike cleaning shrimp. To save some time and "ickyness," ask the seafood department to clean the shrimp for you. They normally only charge an extra $2.00 per pound and it's worth the money!

Tony Stewart, driver of the No. 20 Home Depot Chevrolet, was the 2002 and 2005 NASCAR NEXTEL Cup champion.

18

ROASTED JALAPEÑO PEPPER DIP

Mike and I have a dear friend, Vickie Brawley, who always gives me the absolute best ideas for cooking. She's so amazing that she should have her own catering and special-event business. Her husband, Billy, is also a close friend, as well as a professional scammer on the golf course with my husband! When the boys are out playing eighteen holes, Vickie and I will exchange new recipes and prepare a meal for Mike and Billy. Afterward, the boys argue over putts from their round while we all relax with a glass of wine and some tasty appetizers.

After Vickie taught me this dish, I made it nearly every weekend as an appetizer at the race track. Goat cheese is an excellent switch from your regular cheese-based dip.

INGREDIENTS:

12 jalapeños, seeded and cut into thin strips
2 tablespoons butter
2 tablespoons olive oil
1 garlic clove, chopped
4 ounces goat cheese, crumbled
Tortilla chips or crackers, for serving

PREPARATION:

Preheat the oven to 350°F.

In a skillet over medium heat, cook jalapeño strips in butter and olive oil, stirring, until soft, 3 to 5 minutes. Add the garlic and continue to cook, stirring, for a few more minutes.

Remove from the skillet and place in a small, shallow baking dish. Sprinkle the goat cheese clumps on top of the peppers.

Bake for 30 minutes.

Serve with tortilla chips or crackers.

Makes 2 to 4 servings.

Erin Crocker, driver of the No. 98 Evernham Motorsports Dodge, began her career at the age of seven, racing quarter midgets.

INSIDER RECIPE · ERIN CROCKER

MEXICAN CRUNCH MIX

Erin Crocker is one lucky lady. She was the first female to join the Evernham Motorsports driver development program in 2005. The first and only female ever to win a World of Outlaws race, she now has Cheerios, Betty Crocker, and Hamburger Helper sponsoring her racing efforts in the Craftsman Truck Series, ARCA RE/MAX Series, and NASCAR Busch Grand National Series. Obviously, Erin keeps pretty busy racing, but she also manages to throw together a few of her favorite treats at the track.

INGREDIENTS:

8 cups Corn Chex cereal

4 cups corn chips

2 cups bite-size cheese crackers

One 3.5-ounce bag Pop Secret butter-
   flavored microwave popcorn, popped

3 tablespoons butter, melted

⅓ cup grated Parmesan cheese

One 1 ¼-ounce package Old El Paso taco seasoning mix

PREPARATION:

In a 2-gallon resealable food-storage plastic bag, mix together the cereal, corn chips, crackers, and popcorn. Drizzle with the melted butter. Seal and shake the bag until mixture is evenly coated.

Add the Parmesan cheese and taco seasoning mix. Seal the bag and shake until mixture is evenly coated.

Makes twenty-six 4-ounce servings.

THREE-INGREDIENT CHICKEN DIP

This is by far the easiest and quickest dip to make: It only has three ingredients, plus crackers, for serving. There is no cooking involved, and the taste is magnificent. The recipe came from our good friend Vickie Brawley, who also enjoys throwing together a meal or party for her many friends in racing. If some unexpected guests drop in—or in my case, ten hungry pit crewmembers—you can throw this together and be a winner.

INGREDIENTS:

One 8-ounce package cream cheese
One 9 ¾-ounce can premium chunk white chicken
One 1-ounce packet dry ranch dressing seasoning
Crackers, for serving

PREPARATION:

Allow the cream cheese to soften at room temperature (if you are in a hurry, you can put in the microwave on low for 15 second intervals, but don't overheat!).

Mix together the cream cheese, chicken and seasoning in a bowl and put in refrigerator to chill.

Serve with crackers.

Makes 4 to 6 servings.

CREW TIP

You can leave the dip in a bowl or form it into a ball and wrap with plastic wrap to set in the refrigerator. You can also use light cream cheese and it will not change the flavor or consistency.

SWEET AND SOUR MEATBALLS

When Kenny and Kim Wallace want to entertain their race team, they will serve up this favorite hors d'oeuvre while waiting for some juicy steaks to come off the grill. During the Charlotte race, it's not unusual for the Wallaces to have twenty-plus guests staying at their home, so Kim will make the meatballs ahead in preparation for the big race. It's a family recipe that Kim's been making for twenty years, and it's still a big hit!

INGREDIENTS:

Meatball Mixture:

2 pounds ground beef

4 tablespoons Worcestershire sauce

¾ cup Quaker oats

1 onion, chopped

Salt

Pepper

Sauce Mixture:

2 cups ketchup

6 tablespoons vinegar

1 cup water

½ cup sugar

1 garlic clove, chopped

2 tablespoons cornstarch

PREPARATION:

Preheat the oven to 350°F.

To make the meatballs: Combine all of the ingredients and roll into 2-inch balls. Place the balls in an 11-by-7-by-2-inch baking pan and bake for 30 minutes.

To make the sauce: Combine all of the ingredients in a saucepan and bring just to a boil, then remove from heat. Pour the sauce over the meatballs and bake for an additional 20 minutes.

Makes 4 to 6 servings.

CREW TIP

Place frilled toothpicks in each meatball and place onto a platter to serve.

23

HAMBALLS

One of the more unique culinary presentations in the Cup garage is managed by Ken Enck of Enck's Custom Catering. While working as a weekend warrior and chef for a race team in 1995, he noticed that all the teams spent long hours in the NASCAR garage with only snacks available to them. Ken found a sponsor in Weber Grills, among various other companies, and set up a massive outdoor kitchen to feed race teams. They now serve breakfast, lunch, and sometimes even dinner to thirty-four teams during each event. It's a lot of work, and many hours spent cooking and serving the teams, but the service is superb and the variety of food choices is vast. Hamballs are a favorite for many because they are easy to eat on the go.

INGREDIENTS:

Hamballs:

1 pound fresh ground pork

1 pound cured ham, ground

1 cup bread crumbs

1 large egg

1 teaspoon salt

⅛ teaspoon pepper

¾ to 1 cup milk

¾ cup brown sugar

Glaze:

¾ cup brown sugar

1 teaspoon dry mustard

¼ cup water

½ cup vinegar

PREPARATION:

Preheat the oven to 350°F.

To make the hamballs: Mix all of the ingredients together in large bowl. Shape into small balls (or shape into a loaf).

Bake the hamballs for 30 to 45 minutes. (To make a loaf instead of balls, bake for 1 ½ hours.)

To make the glaze: Mix ingredients together in a saucepan, and bring just to a boil. Halfway through the cooking process, pour half of the glaze over the hamballs (or loaf), and reserve the rest of the glaze to cover the top(s) just before serving.

Makes 4 to 6 servings.

Enck's Custom Catering are well known for their impressive spreads, like this one at the 2006 Auto Club 500 in Fontana, California.

ASIAN GRILLED WINGS

My sister, Tami Queen, shared this recipe with me a few years back. She takes her time dicing and chopping her way toward a perfect meal, but I tend to just throw things together because I never know when we'll need to race off to someplace new—and also because I am rather impatient and hate measuring anything! This is one of those thrown-together recipes that can serve as an appetizer or a main course.

INGREDIENTS:

One 12-ounce jar apricot preserves
1 cup soy sauce
2 cloves garlic, minced
1 teaspoon ground ginger
4-5 pounds chicken wings, or wings and drumsticks mixed
Liquid smoke

PREPARATION:

Mix all of the ingredients together except the liquid smoke in a large bowl. Cover with plastic wrap or a lid and allow to marinate in a refrigerator for at least 4 hours, preferably overnight.

Prepare a grill. Grill the chicken over medium heat until done. Add liquid smoke to taste. You can also bake these at 350°F for 45 minutes to 1 hour. Turn the broiler on at the end to make them crispy.

Makes 4 to 6 servings.

SPEED TIP

I buy the little jars of fresh minced garlic, usually found in the produce department of your local grocery store—it really saves the time involved peeling and chopping garlic. Plus your hands don't smell all day and night!

BACON THINGIES

Jenna Robinson's husband, Clay, works at Hendrick Motorsports and gave her nontraditional rumaki this unique name—which I think is much more attention-grabbing. Jenna notes that traditional rumaki calls for rolled liver, so she usually gets big thanks for making them this way instead. I second that!

INGREDIENTS:

1 pound thick-cut, maple-flavored bacon
One 8-ounce can whole water chestnuts
Toothpicks
2-3 tablespoons brown sugar

PREPARATION:

Preheat the oven to 375°F.

Cut the bacon slices and water chestnuts in half. Roll half of a water chestnut into a half piece of bacon and stick a toothpick through the middle. Continue until all of the chestnuts are rolled.

Line the "bacon thingies" in an 11-by-13-inch baking dish. Bake for 30 minutes.

Carefully pour off any excess grease and sprinkle with the brown sugar.

Put back in the oven for 20 minutes, or until the bacon is crisp and the brown sugar is melted.

Makes 4 to 6 servings.

CREW TIP

You can prepare these ahead of time, but make sure you serve them hot. Any thick-cut bacon will do, but if it's not maple flavored, you'll need more brown sugar. The pan will get rather messy, so after you remove your food, fill the pan with hot water and soak a fabric softener sheet in it overnight. In the morning, it'll be much easier to clean.

I would just purchase a foil baking tray and pitch the pan. But that's just me—I hate scrubbing messy pans!

"MANLY" NACHOS

Another killer recipe from my sister—or as I call her, "Sissy." I wanted to call the recipe Sissy's Nachos, but thought some of you male diehard race fans may not try it because of the name, so I renamed them "manly" because it requires a lot of good beef. In fact, that's what makes these nachos extraordinary. The trick to this recipe is cooking the beef roast all day in a crockpot!

INGREDIENTS:

1 large beef roast
4 beef bouillon cubes, or beef broth
Two 16-ounce jars (one hot and one mild) Old El Paso salsa or picante sauce
One 15-ounce bag tortilla chips
One 8-ounce bag shredded Mexican blended cheese
One 2 ¼-ounce can sliced black olives
Jalapeño peppers
Shredded lettuce
Sour cream
Scallions, chopped
Tomatoes, diced

PREPARATION:

Place the roast in your crockpot and pour in enough water to submerge half of the roast. Add beef bouillon cubes and let cook, covered and on Slow, for 4 hours.

Remove and shred the meat. Remove most of the broth from the crockpot and place the shredded meat back into the pot, along with the salsa. Put the lid back on and allow to simmer and complete cooking for an additional 1 to 1 ½ hours.

You can use the additional meat in the crockpot for soft tacos or quesadillas to accompany your nachos!

Preheat the oven to 375°F. When you are ready to serve the nachos, spread the tortilla chips on a cookie sheet and layer them with beef, cheese, olives, and your desired amount of peppers. Bake until the cheese is melted, about 10 minutes.

Remove from the oven and layer with lettuce, sour cream, scallions, and tomatoes.

Makes 4 to 6 servings.

MARINATED COLD SHRIMP

This is a big hit for any gathering. It only takes about five minutes to make, and can be prepared up to three or four hours beforehand. I got the recipe from a friend after sampling it at her Christmas Eve gathering, and I made it for a special media dinner held at our motor coach, to kick off the 2005 Craftsman Truck Series season. Our race team surprised me by coming over to the coach while I was preparing dinner. I felt guilty not offering them a snack, so I snuck them a large bowl of this shrimp. It's now requested every race after qualifying. The guys on the crew even asked for this recipe—it's that good!

INGREDIENTS:

2 pounds cooked shrimp, deveined and tails off
1 cup mayonnaise
1 cup horseradish
2 teaspoons lemon juice
½ teaspoon kosher salt

1 teaspoon dry mustard
One 2 ¼-ounce can sliced black olives
One 8-ounce can sliced water chestnuts
8-12 small cherry tomatoes

PREPARATION:

Combine all the ingredients and mix together well. Best if marinated overnight.

Makes 4 to 6 servings.

SPEED TIP

I use frozen shrimp for this dish. When I am ready to prepare the recipe, I place the frozen shrimp in a colander and thaw using cold water.

GREEN CHILI AND BEEF PINWHEELS

I'm always searching for bite-sized snacks to serve at the track—preferably something that won't make a mess because the crewmembers work hard and rarely get time to sit down and eat during the day. These tasty wheels have a lot of flavor, as well as a little kick. They will be a hit at any of your race-day parties, too!

INGREDIENTS:

One 2-ounce package dried chipped beef
One 8-ounce package of cream cheese, softened at room temperature
1 can diced green chilies
Two 12-inch flour tortillas

PREPARATION:

Slice and dice the chipped beef. In a bowl, mix together the beef, cream cheese, and green chilies.

Spread the cream cheese mixture evenly over each tortilla. Don't overfill—make sure you can roll each tortilla without the mixture spilling out. Roll and slice into ½-inch bites.

Refrigerate before serving.

Makes 4 to 6 servings.

CREW TIP

To make slicing the rolls a lot easier, allow them to sit in the refrigerator for it least one hour. You can also use low-fat cream cheese for this recipe without disturbing the flavor.

Chemung, New York native Todd Bodine and his wife, Lynn, pose with the Skinners.

INSIDER RECIPE 🏁 **TODD BODINE**

BODINE DIP

When Todd Bodine, driver of the No. 30 Germain Toyota in the NASCAR Craftsman Truck Series (or the driver better known as "The Onion") was a little boy, he would devour this special chip dip every Christmas Eve—and yes, the recipe includes a little something to do with onion! His grandfather would make the dip for their annual holiday get-together, and Todd later convinced his mother to teach him how to make his favorite treat.

Todd's recipe originally called for "⅛ inch of garlic salt in a cap." Figuring only race-car drivers or fabricators would know how much that was, I convinced my husband to show me the measurement. It equals about one teaspoon.

INGREDIENTS:

Two 8-ounce packages cream cheese
1 teaspoon onion salt
1 teaspoon garlic salt

½–1 cup milk
Potato chips, for serving

PREPARATION:

In a bowl, let the cream cheese soften at room temperature (this makes it easier to mix).

Mix the onion salt and garlic salt together with the cream cheese. While beating the mixture, add milk until the dip is the desired thickness.

Serve with potato chips.

Makes 4 to 6 servings.

TOYOTA
TOYOTA RACING DEVELOPMENT
TRD
BOSCH
Spark Plugs
GOODYEAR
RED HORSE
RACING
Miller
sparco

TEXAS HOT SAUCE

Craftsman Truck Series driver David Starr is a fan favorite in his home state of Texas, so it was no surprise that he provided a recipe for his preferred hot sauce, which was given to him by his mother.

INGREDIENTS:

5 large tomatoes
5-7 tomatillos (they look like small green tomatoes), papery husks removed
3-5 serrano peppers (depending on how spicy you prefer)
One 10-ounce can Rotel Mexican Festival diced tomatoes with lime and cilantro
1 tablespoon chopped onion, or more if desired
Salt
Tortilla chips, for serving

33

PREPARATION:

Boil the tomatoes, tomatillos, and peppers for 15 minutes. (You may have to remove the tomatillos first—they tend to soften faster than the tomatoes).

When cool, peel the tomatoes, and mix them together with the tomatillos and peppers in a blender. Add the can of Rotel tomatoes and blend well. Add the chopped onions and blend longer to combine all ingredients thoroughly.

Return the mixture to the saucepan, bring to a boil and cook for 10 minutes.

Remove from the heat and let cool. Add salt to taste. Serve with tortilla chips.

Makes 4 to 6 servings.

David Starr made his first start in 1998 and got his first win in 2002, at Las Vegas Motor Speedway.

BOBBY HAMILTON'S HOT COUNTRY HAM DIP

Bobby Hamilton not only drives a truck in the NASCAR Craftsman Truck Series, he also owns the one that he steers every weekend, as well as three more! Amanda Jones works for Bobby Hamilton Racing, based out of Tennessee, and gave me this recipe. She manages public relations for the teams and told me this is one of Bobby's favorites. The dip was first made for a lunch at the race shop, and quickly became a staple at all their races.

INGREDIENTS:

Two 8-ounce packages cream cheese, softened at room temperature
1 cup sour cream
1 cup cooked and chopped Clifty Farm country ham
½ cup finely minced onion
½ teaspoon garlic powder
1 cup pecans
1 ½ tablespoons butter
½ teaspoon Worcestershire sauce
Crackers or raw vegetables, for serving

34

PREPARATION:

Preheat the oven to 350°F.

Combine softened cream cheese, sour cream, chopped ham, onion, and garlic powder in small bowl. Place in an 8-by-8-inch baking dish.

In a skillet, cook the pecans, stirring, in the butter and Worcestershire sauce over medium heat until lightly browned, about 3 minutes. Sprinkle the pecans over the ham mixture.

Bake for 20 minutes.

Serve hot with crackers or raw vegetables.

Makes 4 to 6 servings.

CREW TIP

This can also be served cold. You may also premix at home and warm it up once you get to the track! Also, you can find Clifty Farm country ham at cliftyfarm.com.

JESSICA'S BRUSCHETTA

Jessica Skarpalezos, the longtime sweetheart of NASCAR driver Steve Park, is an awesome cook. Mike and I have had the pleasure of traveling with Steve and Jessica for a few summers now in our motor coaches, caravanning to races all over the country. We have a couple of things in common: our love for our dogs and an enjoyment of cooking. We've even had some fun experimenting with new foods and culinary creations. Whenever we plan a cookout at the race track, I beg Jessica to make her bruschetta. It's always perfect!

INGREDIENTS:

3-4 large tomatoes, chopped

½ large red onion, diced

Fresh basil leaves, chopped

2 tablespoons extra virgin olive oil

1 tablespoon balsamic vinegar

Pinch sugar

1 loaf French bread, cut on the diagonal

5-6 garlic cloves, peeled

Freshly grated Parmesan cheese, optional

Salt

Pepper

PREPARATION:

Combine the tomatoes, onion, basil, olive oil, vinegar, and sugar in a bowl and refrigerate for at least 2 hours.

Preheat the oven to 350°F. Bring the tomato mixture to room temperature.

Drizzle the bread slices with additional olive oil. Bake the bread until it's toasted or golden around the edges, about 5 minutes.

Remove the toast from oven and transfer it to a serving dish. Rub a garlic clove over each piece of toast, grating the garlic lightly. Top each piece of toast slice with a spoonful of tomato mixture. Sprinkle with cheese, and salt and pepper to taste.

Makes 4 to 6 servings.

CREW TIP

In the winter months, use 6-8 Roma tomatoes. For a gourmet twist, add one boiled shrimp or a lump of crabmeat to the top of each bruschetta. For a Mexican twist, simply substitute cilantro for the basil and lime juice for the vinegar, and top with a slice of avocado.

HARVICK MEXI-CALI DIP

I came upon this recipe by borrowing Kevin and DeLana Harvick's motor coach oven one evening at the race track. Kevin drives the No. 29 GM Goodwrench Chevrolet in the NASCAR NEXTEL Cup Series. As I walked in to bake a stromboli, I spotted and smelled a wonderful Mexican dish. So while I waited for my dinner to bake, I invited myself to theirs! It was excellent.

I always laugh when I make this dip; for weeks I thought it was DeLana's recipe, until Kevin politely let me know that he was the chef. Apparently, before DeLana married Kevin, she was sure to let him know that cooking would not be on her agenda! I still tease her about it today, and she still doesn't like to cook.

INGREDIENTS:

One 8-ounce package cream cheese, softened at room temperature
One 3-ounce can chopped green chilies
One 1 ¼-ounce packet taco seasoning
One 8-ounce can Hormel chili beans
One 3-ounce can sliced black olives
1 cup shredded mozzarella cheese
1 cup shredded Colby jack cheese

PREPARATION:

Preheat the oven to 375°F.

Combine the cream cheese with green chilies and taco seasoning. Spread the mixture evenly over the bottom of an 11-by-7-by-2-inch glass baking dish. Layer the mixture with the beans and black olives, and top with the shredded cheeses.

Bake for approximately 20 minutes, or until bubbly.

Makes 4 to 6 servings.

36

Two fans indulge in their pre-race ritual prior to the 2006 Subway Fresh 500, at Phoenix International Raceway.

INSIDER RECIPE ⚑⚑ **DALE JARRETT**

MEXICAN CORN DIP

Dale Jarrett and his coach driver, Mark "Digger" Shook, have been friends since high school, and for twenty years Digger has driven DJ's motor coach to almost every race Dale has entered. It's a true bond between high school buddies that has stood the test of time and the stresses of NASCAR racing. Not only is Digger a great friend to DJ, he is also always good as gold to me every time I see him at the track. There have even been a few times when my dog Opus went missing, and the first place I looked was inside Jarrett's motor coach. Most often I would find him in there, watching television, while both Digger and DJ munched on this dip.

INGREDIENTS:

Two 11-ounce cans Mexican-style corn
One 4.5-ounce can chopped green chilies
One 8-ounce package
  shredded Monterey jack cheese

1 cup mayonnaise
One 1 ¼-ounce package Old El Paso taco seasoning
Tortilla chips, for serving

PREPARATION:

Preheat the oven to 450°F.

Mix all the ingredients together in a 7-by-12-inch baking dish and bake for 20 minutes. Serve with tortilla chips.

Makes 4 to 6 servings.

Mark "Digger" Shook, left, with Dale Jarrett, also serves as pit scorer for the No. 88 UPS Team.

SWISS AND BACON DIP

If you are looking for a "man's" dip, this is it. It has bacon—enough said.

INGREDIENTS:

8 slices center-cut bacon, chopped

8 ounces cream cheese, softened at room temperature

1 ½ cups shredded Swiss cheese

½ cup mayonnaise

2 rounded teaspoons Dijon-style mustard

2 tablespoons horseradish

3 scallions, chopped

½ cup smoked almonds, coarsely chopped

Crackers, celery, and carrot sticks, for serving

PREPARATION:

Preheat the oven to 350°F.

Brown the bacon in a nonstick skillet over medium-high heat. Drain the crisp bacon on paper towels and break into bits.

In a mixing bowl, combine the softened cream cheese, Swiss cheese, mayonnaise, Dijon mustard, horseradish, and scallions with the cooked bacon. Transfer the mixture to an 11-by-7-by-2-inch casserole dish and bake until golden and bubbly at edges, 15 to 18 minutes. Top with the chopped smoked almonds.

Serve with crackers, celery, and carrot sticks.

Makes 4 to 6 servings.

SPEED TIP

If you are in a hurry or confined to a small space—like a motorcoach kitchen—you can use microwaveable bacon. I prefer Hormel's version.

POLE-SITTIN' SALSA

Sitting on the pole isn't just a term for a race team qualifying first. Tom Lilly's uncle created this special salsa and took first place—hence the name! You won't be disappointed.

INGREDIENTS:

25-30 medium tomatoes, peeled
5 green bell peppers, chopped and seeded
4 medium sized onions, peeled and chopped
2 cups red wine vinegar
½ cup lemon juice
7 tablespoons sugar
2 tablespoons salt
3 teaspoons garlic powder
1 teaspoon cumin
2 teaspoons oregano
6-7 jalapeño peppers*
1 chili pepper*
Tortilla chips for serving

PREPARATION:

*This recipe is for mild sauce. For hot sauce, use 10 to 12 jalapeño peppers and 3 chili peppers.

Combine all the ingredients in a large pot and bring them to a boil. Turn down the heat and simmer for 3 to 4 hours, until consistency is to your liking. Serve with tortilla chips.

Makes 8 to 12 servings.

CHAPTER THREE

RACE-WORTHY MAIN COURSES

Some of the best quick minimeals—as well as some hearty meat dishes and scrumptious stews—can be found in this section. I really enjoy throwing a main course together in less than an hour when I'm at the race track. I hope you enjoy some of my personal favorites, many of which can be made in a matter of minutes, along with some of my racing peers' most requested main dishes!

CRABMEAT AU GRATIN

The late Davey Allison was a true NASCAR star who apparently had an appetite for seafood. This recipe was one of Davey's favorites. His wife, Liz, claims he would have eaten this delicious meal every night if she'd fixed it for him! It's a rich blend of crabmeat and cheese, and became a tradition for the Allison family after Davey won a race.

INGREDIENTS:

1 cup finely chopped onion
4 celery stalks, chopped
¼ pound (1 stick) butter
¼ cup flour
One 13-ounce can evaporated milk
2 large egg yolks
1 teaspoon Worcestershire sauce
¼ teaspoon black pepper
1 teaspoon salt
½–¾ cup milk
1 pound white crab meat
1 cup cooked white rice
½ pound Colby cheese, shredded

PREPARATION:

Preheat the oven to 375°F.

In a large saucepan, cook the onion and celery in the butter until soft, about 5 minutes. Blend in the flour and gradually pour in the milk. Add the egg yolks, Worcestershire sauce and seasonings, and cook over medium heat until thick, about 5 minutes.

Add enough additional milk to create a sauce of medium consistency, about 4 to 6 ounces. Stir in the crabmeat and rice. Pour the mixture into a greased 13-by-9-by-2-inch casserole dish.

Sprinkle the cheese on top and bake until hot and bubbly, or about 20 minutes.

Makes 4 to 6 servings.

In addition to supporting local Humane Societies and no-kill animal shelters, the Greg Biffle Foundation, founded by Nicole Lunders (pictured) and Greg Biffle, raised money for Gulf Coast animal shelters after Hurricane Katrina.

INSIDER RECIPE  **NICOLE LUNDERS**

NO. 16 TACO SALAD

Nicole Lunders is the longtime girlfriend of NASCAR NEXTEL Cup star Greg Biffle. He drives the No. 16 Roush Racing Ford, but Nicole is the driver in their home and motor coach kitchens. This unique twist on a taco salad is requested by Greg over and over! When the couple is not racing, they spend time raising money for the Greg Biffle Foundation, a charity that rescues homeless animals.

INGREDIENTS:

1 head lettuce, broken (don't chop!)

2 pounds ground beef or ground turkey, cooked and drained

1 pound grated or shredded Cheddar cheese

3 tomatoes, chopped

3 avocados, peeled, pitted, and chopped

1 large onion, chopped

1 can kidney beans, drained

1 can black olives, drained and chopped

1 small bottle sweet French salad dressing

¼ cup Italian salad dressing

1-2 cups Doritos, crumbled

PREPARATION:

Mix all of the ingredients, except for the Doritos, together in a salad bowl. Top with the crumbled Doritos.

Makes 4 to 6 servings.

INSIDER RECIPE  **TERRY COOK**

POWER BURGER

NASCAR Craftsman Truck Driver Terry Cook drives the No. 10 Power Stroke Diesel Ford, so downing a power burger before every race is essential for the tough truck driver.

INGREDIENTS:

1 pound ground beef or ground turkey
½ small onion, chopped
1 tablespoon Worcestershire sauce

½ teaspoon seasoning salt
1 slice Colby jack cheese per burger
2-4 hamburger buns

PREPARATION:

Prepare a grill.

Combine the meat, onion, Worcestershire sauce, and seasoning salt in large bowl. Form the mixture into patties. Grill the patties over medium heat to your preference.

Top the burgers with cheese and serve on buns.

Makes 2 to 4 servings.

Terry Cook has been racing in the NASCAR Craftsman Truck Series since 1996.
His first win was the 1998 Stevens Bell/Genuine Car Parts 200.

MOM'S MEXICAN CRUNCHY CASSEROLE

Well the name says it all! My mom made this dish one night for herself and brought Mike and me the leftovers. After we ate our dinner, I wrapped up the remaining serving and hid it in the refrigerator for lunch the following day. Mike and I usually have our lunch together, whether we make it at home or go to one of our favorite restaurants, but that day I kept coming up with excuses to stay home and suggested he go with a buddy instead. He caught on to my scam, and told me he would just go home and have the leftover casserole that mom made. Then the race began. I won, and devoured every last bite before Mike could even get through the door. This is a dish worth fighting over! And it's also great the next day.

INGREDIENTS:

1 pound ground beef
1 large onion, diced
½ cup chopped green bell pepper
1 ½ cups cooked long grain rice
2 tablespoons ketchup
¼ teaspoon salt
1 can cream of mushroom soup
1 ½ cups shredded Cheddar cheese
1 cup milk
½ teaspoon ground mustard
1 teaspoon Worcestershire sauce
2 cups cornflakes, crumbled
3 tablespoons butter, melted

PREPARATION:

Preheat the oven to 375ºF.

In a skillet, cook the ground beef over medium heat with the onion and green pepper until brown, about 10 minutes. Drain the grease.

In a large bowl, combine the meat mixture, rice, ketchup, and salt. In another large bowl, mix together the soup, cheese, milk, mustard, and Worcestershire sauce.

Pour the meat mixture into a 10-by-10-by-2-inch glass baking dish, and then cover with soup mixture. Combine the cornflakes and butter and sprinkle over the casserole.

Bake for 35 minutes.

Makes 6 to 8 servings.

SALMON IN MERLOT

Mark Martin is known as one of the greatest race car drivers to ever hold a steering wheel. He is also known for his strict regimen for staying in shape by exercising and eating healthy food. This salmon recipe is great and very simple to make in his motor coach at the race track.

INGREDIENTS:

1 pound salmon fillet
1 cup low sodium soy sauce
½ cup merlot wine
½ teaspoon ground ginger
½ teaspoon pepper

PREPARATION:

Combine all the ingredients in a plastic resealable bag and marinate at least 4 hours, preferably overnight.

Prepare a grill. Grill the salmon over medium heat until done, about 10 minutes.

Makes 2 to 4 servings.

Mark Martin has won five IROC titles and finished second in NASCAR NEXTEL Cup standings four times.

CHEESY CHICKEN POT PIE

Katie Kenseth, wife of NASCAR champion driver Matt Kenseth, knows a thing or two about making this scrumptious pot pie–not because she claims to be a professional chef, but because it took her a few attempts to make it right! This is Matt's favorite meal, so when Katie first started cooking for him, she was determined to perfect it. One afternoon Matt called Katie on his way home from a long day at the race shop. She was so proud to tell her husband she was cooking his favorite meal—the only problem was, her white sauce was a disaster. After three attempts and a burnt mess, Matt's dinner ended up in the garbage. When he got home he found Katie grilling hot dogs and asked her, "What happened to my pot pie?" Katie pointed to the garbage, and he didn't say another word. That night they enjoyed Katie's gourmet hot dogs.

The good news is that Katie has since perfected the white sauce and is willing to share a great tip: When you attempt this pot pie for the first time, use the microwave!

INGREDIENTS:

One 9-inch frozen pie crust

3 tablespoons butter

3 tablespoons flour

½-1 teaspoon dry mustard

½-1 teaspoon dried sage

1 cup milk

2 chicken bouillon cubes, crumbled

1 cup shredded Cheddar cheese

3 cups mixed vegetables, drained and cooked (or use
   frozen variety and prepare according to package)

2 cups potatoes, peeled, cubed, and cooked

3 cups cooked cut-up chicken

PREPARATION:

Preheat the oven to 400°F.

Invert the frozen pie shell onto sheet of plastic wrap. Cover the shell with another sheet of plastic wrap and let thaw, or allow refrigerated pie crust to come to room temperature according to package directions.

In a 3-quart saucepan over medium heat, melt the butter. Stir in the flour, mustard, and sage, and stir until smooth.

Gradually stir in the milk and bouillon cubes. Cook, stirring constantly, until the mixture boils and thickens. (You can also use the microwave, using a microwave-safe bowl, just remember to heat in 2-minute increments and stir after each increment.)

Add the cheese and stir until it is melted. Remove the mixture from heat and stir in the chicken, vegetables, and potatoes. Pour the mixture into a 2-quart round casserole dish.

Flatten the pie crust and seal any tears by pressing the dough together. Place the crust over the filling, folding the edge under to form a rim. Cut slits in the top of the crust to vent steam.

Bake for 35 minutes or until crust is browned. Let stand for 10 minutes before serving.

Makes 6 servings.

Check your crust after baking for 15 minutes. If the edges are browning too quickly, cover with strips of foil.

To avoid cooking and cubing potatoes, buy the canned version of cubed white potatoes. Also, cut up a rotisserie chicken to avoid cooking the meat.

SALMON SUITED FOR A CHAMPION

Back in the day, three-time NASCAR champion Darrell Waltrip would tell you that his favorite meal was a big bowl of white beans and cornbread. Now however, for his race track meal, the Fox Television announcer watches his carbs by enjoying a healthy salmon fixed specially on the grill. This is one of the dishes his motor-coach driver, Clifford "Smitty" Smith, will grill for DW after a long day in the broadcast booth. Before he digs in, I wonder if DW shouts, "Boogity-Boogity-Boogity!"

INGREDIENTS:

1 pound salmon fillet
1 unpeeled zucchini, sliced
1 unpeeled yellow squash, sliced
2 tablespoons olive oil
1 lemon
Salt
Pepper

PREPARATION:

Place the salmon on a large sheet of aluminum foil, and surround it with the zucchini and squash slices.

Drizzle the olive oil and squeeze the juice of the lemon over the fish and vegetables. Salt and pepper to taste. Fold and close the aluminum foil to allow steaming.

Prepare a grill and then, as Smitty says, "Whop it on the grill!" Cook over medium heat until the salmon is done, about 10 minutes.

Makes 2 to 3 servings.

CREW TIP

I found that if you like a little kick added to your salmon, sprinkle some crushed red pepper and Cracker Girl seasoning—yum!

CRAWFORD OYSTER STEW

NASCAR Craftsman Truck Series driver Rick Crawford has been racing in the NASCAR tough series since its inception in 1995, and he's one of the favorites in the series. He also has a pretty good recipe to share from his Alabama roots. Rick says this oyster stew is the best in the South, even though this Southern gentleman also claims the warranty is still good on his stove at home. Rick adds, "I tend to burn cornflakes!"

INGREDIENTS:

1 ½-2 pounds fresh oysters
¼ pound (1 stick) butter
4 cups milk
Salt
Pepper

PREPARATION:

Clean the oysters and pat them dry.

Sear the oysters in a pan with 4 tablespoons (or more, if desired) of butter. Set the oysters aside.

Warm the milk with 2 tablespoons of the butter. Salt and pepper the milk mixture to taste. Add the oysters and simmer until they are desired tenderness, or about 10 minutes.

Makes 2 to 4 servings.

CREW TIP

Rick adds, "This stew is quite tasty with saltine crackers, and don't be afraid of the pepper!"

NO. 22 CAT CAR CHILI

Gina Mayercheck took on a new job in February 2006 cooking for all the Bill Davis Racing crewmen—and also me, when I sneak over to eat lunch during practices! This chili recipe originally came from the Betty Crocker cookbook, but Gina made a few changes to create her own variation. Gina made this (for the first time) during Speedweeks in Daytona, and the crew loved the results. Coming from a large Italian family, this team chef learned one valuable lesson from her mother: Always start with good ingredients! The quantities have been increased in order to feed all of BDR, so this is a great one for your tailgate crew.

INGREDIENTS:

8-9 pounds ground beef
4 onions, chopped
8 stalks celery, chopped
Four 28-ounce cans diced tomatoes
One 28-ounce can tomato sauce
24 ounces water
One 6-ounce can tomato paste
8 teaspoons Worcestershire sauce
8 tablespoons chili powder
5 tablespoons salt
4 teaspoons garlic powder
2 teaspoons red pepper sauce
Six 15-ounce can kidney beans

PREPARATION:

In a very large pot, cook the ground beef over medium heat until brown, about 10 minutes. Drain the grease, remove the beef and set aside. In the same large pot, cook the onion and celery over medium heat, stirring, until soft, about 5 minutes. Add the beef, tomatoes, tomato sauce, water, paste, Worcestershire sauce, red pepper sauce, and spices, and bring to a boil. Reduce the heat and simmer for 1 hour.

Add the kidney beans and simmer for an additional 15 minutes.

Makes 10 to 12 servings.

Cooking for a race crew can be a tough task, but Gina Mayercheck manages to stir with a smile.

COMPTON MAC AND CHEESE

Vickie Compton is the wife of NASCAR Busch Series driver Stacy Compton; she's also one of my best buddies in the series and probably the sweetest woman in the NASCAR garage. We often joke that it's impossible for her to even make a mean face at anyone. I tried really hard to get Vickie to share her famous "cola" cookie recipe but she gave me her mac and cheese instead, explaining that it's Stacy and her daughter Olivia's favorite Compton dish.

I still have to share her "cola" cookie story—just to make you laugh! At the age of ten, Vickie started experimenting in the kitchen. One afternoon she chose to make some cookies, and the recipe called for a couple tablespoons of soda. Being raised in Virginia, this Southern belle only knew one soda, and that was Coca-Cola, so in went the Coca-Cola and out came some really sticky cookies and a cookie sheet for the garbage container! Don't worry folks, Vic's mom explained the difference between baking soda and Coca-Cola to Vickie, and today she can proudly make cookies to rival any baking diva. Now you know why you don't want the "cola" cookie recipe and should try this scrumptious mac and cheese instead!

56

INGREDIENTS:

One 16-ounce box macaroni noodles
One 16-ounce box of Velveeta cheese
2 tablespoons butter
Pinch of salt
2–3 cups milk, or heavy cream

PREPARATION:

Preheat oven to 350°F.

Boil the macaroni noodles until al dente. Drain the noodles and set them aside.

In a casserole dish, cube the Velveeta, and combine it with the butter and salt. Pour in enough milk to just cover the cheese and butter. Bake the mixture until cheese is melted, about 10 minutes. Add the noodles.

Stir the mixture until creamy, adding more milk to cover the noodles again. Stir the mixture one last time and bake for 30 minutes.

Makes 2 to 4 servings.

CREW TIP

For a creamier texture use heavy cream with your milk. For a lower-fat version, stick with skim milk only.

EASY STROMBOLI

My best friend, Amy Plumley, gave me this recipe over the phone one evening when I was trying to impress Mike's taste buds. He loves sausage, and this stromboli became a hit in the Skinner kitchen on and off the road.

INGREDIENTS:

1 onion, chopped

One 8-ounce package of fresh sliced mushrooms

2 tablespoons olive oil

1 to 1 ½ pounds of ground sausage, some hot and some Italian flavor

2 teaspoons garlic powder

Dash or two of Italian seasoning

Two 10-ounce tubes Pillsbury pizza dough

1 ½ ounces sliced pepperoni

6 ounces Italian-flavored tomatoes, chopped

One 8-ounce bag of shredded Italian-blend cheese

4-6 tablespoons pizza sauce, or your favorite marinara sauce

½-1 cup fresh grated Parmesan cheese

PREPARATION:

Preheat the oven to 375ºF.

In a skillet, cook the onions and mushrooms in the olive oil over medium heat, stirring, until soft, about 5 minutes, and set aside.

In another large skillet, brown the sausage. While cooking the sausage, add the garlic powder and a couple shakes of Italian seasoning. Drain the sausage and combine it with the onions and mushrooms.

57

You can create a ton of varieties with this dish—pepperoni only, veggie, etc. Most of the time I will make four total, with each one a different style.

Roll out the pizza doughs onto a greased cookie sheet. Place the sausage mixture on one side of each piece of the dough. Layer the mixture with a few pepperoni slices. Add 2 to 3 spoonfuls of chopped tomatoes and top off with shredded cheese.

Fold the other half of the dough over to cover your filling, and press the seams together. (Be careful not to overfill!) Sprinkle Italian seasoning onto the dough.

Bake for 15 to 20 minutes. Don't overcook the dough—it should be just browning when you remove from the oven. While the dough is baking, warm up the pizza sauce or marinara.

When ready to serve, slice the stromboli lengthwise and place a spoonful of sauce over the top of each serving. Top with Parmesan cheese.

Makes 2 to 4 servings.

MEARS' MEXICAN POZOLE
(MEXICAN STEW)

The Mears family is famous in the racing world for a variety of racing—from NASCAR to open-wheel, off-road, and Grand Am Sports Car events. We on the NASCAR circuit are lucky to know Roger and Carol Mears, parents of No. 42 NASCAR NEXTEL Cup driver, Casey Mears. They are truly two of the friendliest and most gregarious folks at the track. Before Casey was the famous racing Mears, his dad was known as one of the greatest off-road racers in history. Casey's uncle Rick is still considered to be one of the greatest open-wheel drivers of all time. The Mears gang obviously has spent a lot of time at the track!

These days, Roger drives his son's motor coach to every race on the NASCAR circuit, while Carol joins the family caravan and still gets to cook a little for her son. This recipe is one of the family's favorites, as it reminds them of their small getaway in Bahai de Los Angeles. This is a real Mexican treat!

INGREDIENTS:

Meat:

1 onion, chopped	2 small cans white hominy
2 garlic cloves, minced	6 tablespoons ground chili piquin powder
1 sprig cilantro or 2 pinches dried cilantro	1 ½ teaspoon ground oregano
Salt	
10 cups water or chicken broth	
3 pounds boneless pork butt	
14 cups water	

Sauce:

10-12 dried chilies (remove seeds and membranes)	4 garlic cloves
½ cup water	7 tablespoons oil
¼ onion, chopped	

Shredded cabbage, sliced radishes, and lime wedges for garnish
Tortillas, for serving

PREPARATION:

To make the meat: In a skillet, cook the onion, garlic, cilantro and salt (to taste), over medium heat, stirring, until the onion is translucent, about 5 minutes. Cover the mixture with the 10 cups of water or chicken broth. Simmer the stock for 20 minutes and set aside.

In a stockpot, boil the pork butt in the 14 cups of water, then simmer until the pork is very tender and shredding, or about 1 hour. Add the hominy to the pork butt and cook for 30 minutes.

Remove and shred the pork, then return it to the pot. Add the stock of onion, garlic, salt, and cilantro. Add the chili piquin powder and oregano. (When adding the chili piquin, do a little at time to make sure it has a great flavor but doesn't get too spicy.)

To make the sauce: In a pot or large bowl, cover the chilies with hot water and soak for 30 minutes, then drain. In a blender, puree the chilies with the water, onion, and garlic.

Heat the oil in a skillet over high heat and add the chili sauce puree. Reduce the heat to medium and cook for 5 minutes. Lower the heat and cook for 10 minutes. Combine the chili sauce puree with the pozole.

Garnish the pozole with the shredded cabbage, radishes, and limes. Serve with warm tortillas.

Makes 4 to 6 servings.

In 2006, Casey Mears became the first ever full-time NASCAR driver to win the annual Rolex 24 Hours of Daytona.

CHICKEN AND DUMPLINGS
[LIKE MOM MAKES]

Not every weekend can be sunny and beautiful—that's why we need a few comfort-food recipes for those weekends of cold rain and muddy infields. This recipe is just the ticket. It's also a meal you can prepare before leaving your home for your tailgate party or campsite.

INGREDIENTS:

4 boneless chicken breasts
¼ pound (1 stick) butter
2 cups self-rising flour
1 cup milk
1 large can (46-50 ounces) chicken broth

PREPARATION:

Cut the chicken into cubes and cook in a skillet over medium heat until done, about 10 minutes.

In a small pot, melt the butter and pour it into a large mixing bowl. Add the flour and milk and mix until dough forms.

In a large stockpot, heat chicken broth over high heat until boiling. Drop tablespoon-sized balls of dough into the broth. Reduce the heat to low, cover, and let cook for 20 minutes. After 15 minutes, add the cooked chicken.

Variation: Stir in some cooked veggies, such as carrots, peas, and corn, to make a stew.

Makes 4 to 6 servings.

To cut cooking time, purchase a rotisserie chicken and shred. Do not use the skin!